D1384390

Basic Soap Recipe

1. Cut soap in 1" chunks, place in microwave bowl or double boiler.

2. Heat in microwave at 20 second intervals until melted.

3. Add a very small amount of color and fragrance.

4. Stir melted soap slowly with a stick or spoon to prevent bubbles.

5. Set aside for 3 to 4 minutes to cool, until steaming stops.

6. Pour slowly into mold.

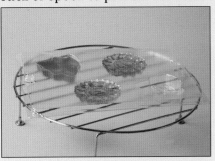

7. Cool from 10 to 30 minutes until hard.

8. Pop out of mold. For easy removal, place in refrigerator for a few minutes, then run hot water on bottom of mold.

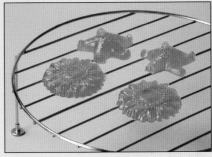

9. Cure on a rack. Air dry about 2 weeks.

Basic Materials

Soap
Transparent and opaque (transparent + powdered milk can substitute for opaque but does not work as well as opaque soap)

Additives
Herbs - sage, chamomile, oregano, cloves, cinnamon, nutmeg, mint
Flowers - Hibiscus, rose, chamomile, calendula, lavender, sunflower
Fruit - lemon, orange, lime, avocado, strawberry
Vegetables - carrots, cucumber, lettuce
Toys
Oils - olive oil, vitamin E, safflower, baby
Honey
Powdered milk
Buttermilk

Colorants
Soap colorants, crayons, spices (cinnamon makes a good brown as well as ground coffee), candle colorants

Fragrant Scents
Scented oils, herbs, spices, fruit. Do not use alcohol based perfumes. Cinnamon, clove, lemon, jasmine, raspberry, musk, sandalwood, honeysuckle, gardenia, apple, pearberry, lavender, peppermint, vanilla

Tools
Pyrex cup, spoons, craft sticks, microwave oven, microwave bowls, candy, soap or small molds, measuring spoons, mixing bowl, wire whisk, drying rack, sharp knife, small food processor, hand grater

Tips
• If using a large loaf pan or mold, you can make smaller portions with cardboard dividers.
• It is easy to over-color soap, so make small portions of each colored soap and allow to dry. Use these small chunks of colored soaps to color other batches.
• Save all colored scraps in baggies to reuse in other soaps.

Confetti

1. Cut small chunks of colored soap and place in freezer to chill. Melt base soap.

2. Pour half of base soap into mold and add a portion of the small chunks. Allow a skin to form on top.

3. Place second half of small chunks on the skimmed surface. Slowly pour on slightly cooled base soap.

Tips

- Place small soap pieces in the freezer to chill to prevent melting when hot soap is added.

- Make as many layers as desired to spread the confetti pieces throughout the soap.

- Use slightly cooled liquid soap as the base to keep from melting the confetti pieces.

Turtles - Mold 111, Yellow and Brown chunks with Clear background or Brown, Yellow and Green chunks with Clear background

Frogs - White opaque eyes, Green and Yellow chunks with Clear background, or Green and Brown chunks with Clear background

Animal Cracker Soaps - Yellow cookie cutter animal, Opaque Light Pink, Light Blue, Light Purple and White cubes with Clear background

Confetti Bar - Small pieces of Yellow, White, Blue and Green curls with Clear background

Bear - Soap chunks with coffee grounds. Base soap colored with nutmeg and cinnamon (trace amount).

Sun - Mold N47, Marble with cinnamon

Leaf - Mold F87, Milk soap base, Yellow and Red colorant

Shells - Mold N47, Red and Yellow or Blue and Yellow colorant

Butterfly - Mold 88, Marble Yellow and White soap

Dolphin - Mold N47, Marble White and Green soap

Marbling

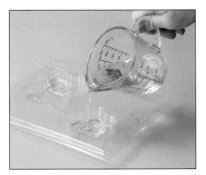

1. Pour base soap into mold.

2. Add one drop of each colorant.

3. Mix with toothpick or craft stick. Do not over-stir.

Embedding Surprises

These soaps can be as much fun as fossil hunting. Make them for party favors, stocking stuffers or just plain fun!

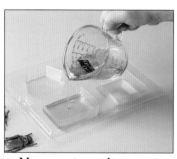

1. Measure to make sure toy is not too tall for mold. Pour a thin, very lightly colored soap into mold as base for toy. Allow skin to form strong enough to hold the toy's weight.

2. Place toy face side down in mold.

3. Cover toy with a slightly darker color for the base.

Bugs - Shavings of Yellow and Coffee Brown soap with a Clear base

Dolphin - Shavings of Yellow, Orange and Brown with Clear base, nutmeg for spots

Kid Pins - Clear + Yellow or Clear + Orange

Treasure Money - Clear + Glitter covered with Amber Yellow + Nutmeg

Tips
• Make hidden messages by writing notes on paper and wrapping with plastic before embedding.
• Embedded soaps make wonderful party favors!

Layers of Colors

Tips for Color Gradation

For best results, use transparent soap and deep molds.

- Mix the darkest color first, making enough to add to Clear soap for lighter colors.
- Pour darkest color first. Allow to cool slightly forming a light skin.
- Add a small amount of Clear soap to your original color. Allow to cool slightly before pouring on first layer to prevent melting the skinned surface. Pour and allow to cool again.
- Repeat as many times as necessary ending with Clear color.
- If gradating in a shallow mold, melt and simultaneously pour the dark color and clear colors very slowly.

Starfish - Mold N47, White with Transparent Green or White with Transparent Blue

Flower - Mold 88, White, Opaque Yellow

Oval - Mold 152, layer Transparent Turquoise with Transparent Purple

Round - Mold 154, layer Transparent Turquoise with Transparent Yellow

Watermelon - Pour small amount of Red, allow to skin over to hold the weight of the seeds. Pour another portion of Red to place the seed made from Coffee grounds soap. Allow to harden completely. Pour Opaque White, allow to harden. Pour Opaque Green.

Hexagon - First layer is soap and corn meal mixed, second layer is Yellow + a few popcorn kernels. (Use colored corn kernels if desired.)

See Tips on page 23.

1. Pour first layer in mold and allow to harden

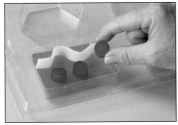

2. Allow soap to cool slightly, pour second layer and cool. Add soap chunks.

3. Pour third layer. Make as many layers as desired.

Cookie Cutter Shapes

Cookie cutter soaps are fun to make for holidays and special occasions.
Or cut small shapes and embed them in clear soap for special effects.

1. Pour soap into a small pan or mold that is large enough to hold cookie cutter. Pour only to depth of cookie cutter. Place cookie cutter in pan while mixture is hot. Allow to harden.

2. Allow to harden, then pull everything out of the pan. Remove cookie cutter and remove soap.

Citrus Slices

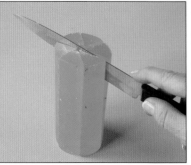

1. Sand outside ends of PVC pipe . Rubber band 8 layers of plastic wrap on one end of 2" pipe. Pour in colored transparent soap, allow to harden.

2. Push soap out end of pipe with a plunger. Cut fruit in half lengthwise. Cut halves in thirds. Do not mix up the sections. Place 8 layers of plastic wrap on work surface. Arrange 6 sections in center of plastic. Keep the soap sections spaced a bit apart. Do not try to be too perfect. Place 3" pipe over sections. Carefully bring plastic wrap up around sides of pipe and secure with the rubber band.

3. Melt and pour Opaque White. Allow to harden. Place in freezer to cool. Remove the soap from the pipe and slice fruit sections.

Tips

- Use Transparent Orange, Yellow and Lime Green soaps for fruit slices.
- Place pipe with hardened soap in freezer to chill to make soap removal easier.
- Remember to let hot white soap cool a bit before pouring around fruit slices so colored portion will not melt.
- Make a plunger with 1½" circle of heavy cardboard and a stick.

Herbal Bars

Contain ingredients that not only cleanse but also condition and heal the skin. Just choose herbs that match your skin type.

Basic Hand Milled Soap Recipe

MATERIALS: ½ cup soap, 2 tablespoons water, 2 tablespoons olive oil, Color, Fragrance

1. Prepare ingredients in three containers: soap cubes, liquids (water, oil & fragrance), and dry ingredients.

- Hand milled soaps have a natural, handmade look.

- The soaps last longer.

- If soap becomes too sudsy while beating, add more oil.

- It requires more colorant to color hand milled soap.

2. Melt cubes of soap in microwave. Allow soap to stop steaming before removing.

3. Add oil, water, botanicals, fragrance and colors to a bowl.

4. Whisk vigorously until the soap thickens to the consistency of heavy cream.

5. Beat until mixture is fluffy (it will look like egg whites). Pour mixture into mold, let harden.

6. Remove shapes from mold and place on a rack to dry. Air dry for 2 weeks.

Additives

Fragrances

- Use any fragrance that is added to candles, soap or pot-pourri.
- Do not use perfumes that are alcohol based. The fragrance will evaporate.
- Fruit Fresh can be added to soaps with fresh fruits and vegetables as a preservative.

Oils

- Olive oil is exceptionally mild and healing to the skin. It causes the soap to be smooth, off white in color and long lasting. Use extra-virgin olive oil available in grocery stores.

- Vitamin E is good to use with vegetables and fruits. It aids in healing and beautifying the skin. Capsules, are less expensive than bottled oil and readily available.
- Almond oil is the best and finest oil for all purpose soap-making. It has a neutral color and is unscented. It is easily absorbed into the skin but is very expensive.
- Castor oil is a mild, pure, natural emollient that penetrates the skin well and is excellent for bath oils. Castor oil is available at pharmacies.
- Other oils are Baby oil which is especially good for bath oils, Cocoa butter, Palm oil, Safflower oil and Coconut oil.

Herbal Bars

Herbal bars add a whole range of sensations to the bath. Not only are these soaps aromatic, they also provide a wide range of healing properties for your skin.

Cornmeal is used as a mild abrasive to help unclog skin pores and absorb oils.

Golden Cornmeal Bar

Add ¼ cup of cornmeal, Yellow coloring and 2 tablespoons of extra water to the Basic Hand Milled Soap Recipe.

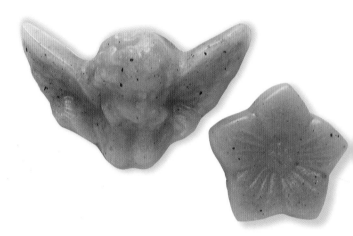

Honey is a natural emollient and milk is a natural cleanser. This age old combination promotes soft, healthy skin.

Milk & Honey Soap

Add 2 tablespoons of powdered milk, 2 tablespoons of honey, 3 tablespoons of water and a dash of nutmeg for color to the Basic Hand Milled Soap Recipe. A little citronella enhances the honey fragrance of this soft soap.

This is a fun and decorative soap that is high in Vitamin A for soft, healthy skin.

Carrot Soap

Slice carrots and blend in a food processor to pulverize. Strain the liquid. Add ¼ cup of carrot pulp in place of water, one medium grated carrot and one tablespoon of Fruit Fresh to the Basic Soap Recipe. Mold.

This soap gently softens sensitive skin.

Oatmeal Soap

Gently fold ¼ cup of oatmeal and cinnamon scent drops into melted soap. Or hand mill the soap.

Cornmeal Bar

Add ¼ cup of cornmeal and 2 tablespoons of extra water to the Basic Hand Milled Soap Recipe.

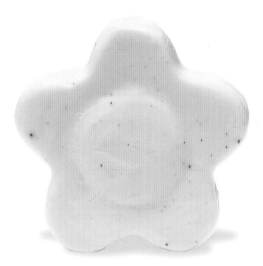

This soap has been used for centuries as a cleanser for soft, sensitive skin.

Buttermilk Soap

Add ¼ cup of buttermilk as a substitute for water, one teaspoon of Fruit Fresh, several drops of peppermint fragrance and a little Yellow colorant to the Basic Hand Milled Soap Recipe. Form in a mold.

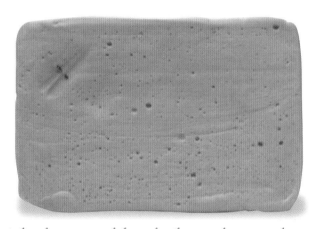

This bar is good for oily skin and is very drying.

Facial Clay Bar

Dissolve 1 to 2 tablespoons of French clay or kaolin and a pinch of Blue colorant shavings in enough water to liquefy. Add to the Basic Hand Milled Soap Recipe.

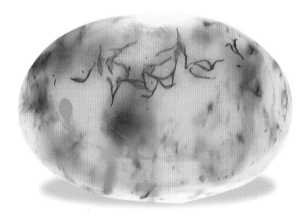

This soap is very soothing, good for inflammation and slightly astringent.

Chamomile Flower Soap

Add ¼ cup of dried chamomile flowers or contents of a tea bag, substitute chamomile tea for water and Yellow coloring to the Basic Soap Recipe.

This soap is soothing to extra sensitive skin and is historically known as a skin softener.

Calendula Flower Soap

Add ¼ cup of fresh or dried calendula petals and Yellow colorant to the Basic Soap Recipe. Add the flowers while stirring as soap begins to thicken. Mold.

Herbal Bars

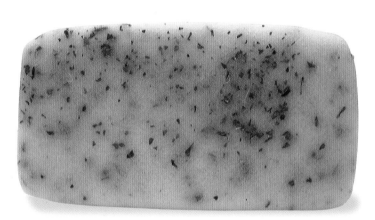

This is a pretty, healing and antiseptic soap.

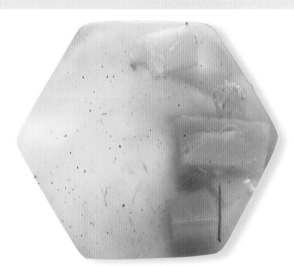

This soap is soft and moisturizing for the skin.

Tea Tree & Oregano Soap

Add 5 drops of tea tree oil and 2 tablespoons of dried oregano to the Basic Hand Milled Soap Recipe.

Avocado Bath Bar

Add one teaspoon of Fruit Fresh and a few avocado chunks to the Basic Soap Recipe. Or mash 2 tablespoon of avocado and add to the Basic Hand Milled Soap Recipe. Chamomile tea flakes and Amber soap shavings may be added for color.

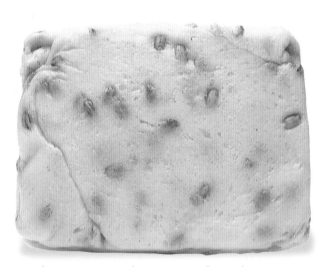

This soap is rich in minerals and vitamins. It soothes, heals and moisturizes sensitive skin.

This soap is healing to the skin. It soothes and prevents wrinkles.

Barley Soap

Add ¼ cup of barley grains and 2 tablespoons of barley cereal boiled in water to the Basic Hand Milled Soap Recipe.

Vitamin E Soap

Add the contents of 6 to 8 vitamin E capsules and fragrance to the Basic Hand Milled Soap Recipe reducing some of the oil. The soap is frothy so stir slowly.

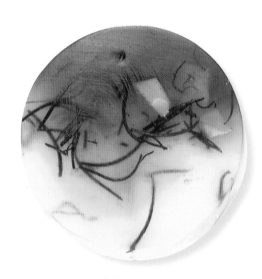

This soap acts as a mild, fresh cleanser and astringent.

Cucumber Soap

Cut a cucumber, remove seeds and blend in a food processor. Add ¼ cup of cucumber as a substitute for water, 2 teaspoons of Fruit Fresh and Green colorant to the Basic Hand Milled Soap Recipe.

This soap is a mild astringent, antiseptic and anti-inflammatory that is stimulating to the skin.

Rosemary Soap

Boil rosemary in ⅛ to ¼ cup of water or use one teaspoon of rosemary oil. Add rosemary and fragrance to the Basic Soap Recipe. Place Opaque White chunks in mold and pour Clear and Dark Transparent Green soap simultaneously to made a gradated color.

These bars are smooth, rich, healing soaps good for all skin types.

Aloe Vera Gel Bar

Add ⅛ cup of aloe vera gel in place of water and part of the oil and Opaque White cubes to the Basic Hand Milled Soap Recipe. Stir very slowly.

This soap absorbs odors from the skin and is a good hand soap for use in the kitchen.

Coffee Bath Bar

Add one tablespoon of unbrewed coffee to the Basic Hand Milled Soap Recipe.

Herbal Bars

Tip for Soaps

• When adding fragrances to hot melted soap, make sure that the hot mixture has cooled off a bit; that way, your fragrance won't burn off.

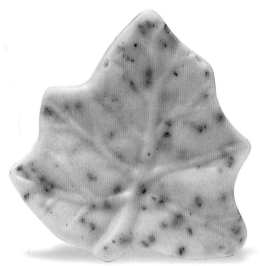

This soap has a fresh, stimulating smell.

Mint Soap

Brew ¼ cup of water with mint leaves. Discard leaves from mint water. Add mint water, ¼ cup of dried mint and 1 to 2 drops of Green colorant to the Basic Hand Milled Soap Recipe. Add dried mint leaves for color.

This soap has antibacterial and astringent qualities.

Sage Soap

Add 3 tablespoons of dried sage to the Basic Hand Milled Soap Recipe. The results are a pretty, natural looking soap.

This soap is a natural soap that warms the skin.

Ginger & Spice Soap

Add 2 teaspoons of powdered ginger and ½ teaspoon of nutmeg to the Basic Hand Milled Soap Recipe.

Tea tree oil is known for its healing properties and antiseptic nature.

Tea Tree Oil Soap

Add 5 drops of tea tree oil, Opaque Light Green and White chunks and a dash of Nutmeg for color to the Basic Soap Recipe. Place a few Amber soap shavings in a mold and pour in the melted soap.

*This soap is an age old skin softener.
Grace Kelly made rose water and used it daily.*

Rose Water Soap

Make petals from a sheet of White soap and freeze. Make rose water by boiling water and adding fresh rose petals. Add ¼ cup of rose water, rose fragrance and one drop of Red colorant to the Basic Soap Recipe. Place petals in mold and add melted soap.

This soap is a sweet, decorative soap.

Cherry Blossom Soap

Make petals from a sheet of White soap and freeze. Make blossom water by boiling water and adding cherry petals. Add ¼ cup of cherry water, cherry fragrance and Red and a little Purple colorant to the Basic Soap Recipe. Place petals in mold and add melted Clear and Red soap simultaneously for gradated color.

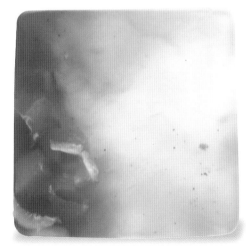

This soap is relaxing, soothing and has antiseptic qualities.

Lavender Soap

Make petals from a sheet of White soap and freeze. Make lavender water by boiling water and adding lavender petals. Add ¼ cup of lavender water, lavender fragrance and one drop of Purple colorant to the Basic Soap Recipe. Place petals in mold and add melted Clear and Lavender soap simultaneously for gradated color.

This soap contains vitamins and is very mild.

Lettuce Leaf Soap

Tear 3 leaves of lettuce, place in food processor with just enough water to liquefy. Add lettuce, one teaspoon of Fruit Fresh and Pale Green colorant to the Basic Hand Milled Soap Recipe.

Herbal Bars

Apricot adds skin softening properties and makes a rich, creamy soap.

Apricot Bar

Add 2 tablespoons of apricot juice or dried apricots, apricot fragrance and Transparent Yellow and Red colorant for a very Light Orange background to the Clear Basic Soap Recipe. Layer Transparent Orange chunks in a loaf pan and add melted soap.

This spicy scented and astringent soap adds zip to your bath.

Cinnamon Stick Soap

Melt Clear soap base and add cinnamon oil and a dash of cinnamon powder. Layer cinnamon sticks in a loaf pan in different directions. Pour melted soap in pan.

Lemon is a fresh, good cleanser. The oil in the peel is an antibacterial and contains high levels of vitamin C.

Lemon Bar

Peel half a lemon and grind the peel. Blend the pulp in a food processor. Add 1/8 cup of lemon, lemon peel, lemon fragrance and Yellow colorant to the Clear Basic Soap Recipe.

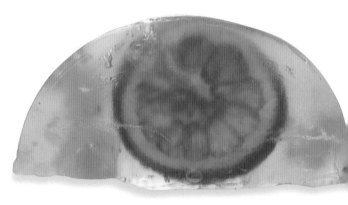

Add Vitamin C as well as the fresh scent of citrus with this orange slice soap.

Orange Splash

Add orange fragrance to the Clear Basic Soap Recipe. Place dried orange slice and a tablespoon of Orange soap chunks in a loaf pan and add melted soap.

Almond soap is a good cleanser and unclogs pores in the face. It is slightly drying and has a fresh nutty smell.

Almond Butterfly Soap

Grind ½ cup of almonds into chucks, remove half and grind remaining nuts into a meal. Add almonds, fragrance and an extra tablespoon of oil to the Basic Hand Milled Soap Recipe. Mold. Almond oil may be substituted for olive oil.

Cloves are an antiseptic but can irritate skin.

Clove Bar

Make a clove tea by steeping cloves in hot water. Add clove tea in place of water and one tablespoon of ground cloves to the Basic Hand Milled Soap Recipe.

This soap is excellent for little boys who play hard.

Gardener's Sand Soap

Use ½ cup of sand and increase the water and oil to ¼ cup in the Basic Hand Milled Soap Recipe. Stir continually until almost hard or the sand will sink.

This is a fun, sunshiny soap.

Sunflower Seed Soap

Steep a sunflower in ½ cup of water. Grind ¼ cup of raw hulled sunflower seeds adding ¼ cup of the sunflower tea. Add seeds, Yellow colorant and sunflower fragrance to the Basic Hand Milled Soap Recipe.

Basic Loaf

Basic Loaf Tips

A basic loaf is a good way to make several slices of the same soap design for gifts.

- Use a loaf mold or a bread loaf pan.
- Prepare all chunks first and cool in the freezer.
- Plan how to arrange the design. The background color needs to be very lightly colored so the design shows.
- Pour first layer, then add chunks when that layer hardens enough to hold them. Repeat until mold is full.

Curls

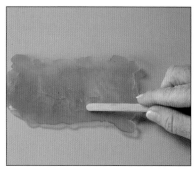

1. Pour melted soap on a smooth, non-stick cookie sheet.

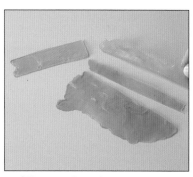

2. Allow to barely set up. Work fast and cut in strips. Remove a strip with a spatula or knife.

3. Curl starting at tight end and roll up. Use only one strip at a time or strips will cool too fast.

If you don't want to make a whole loaf of the same design but want the look of loaf soap, section off a loaf pan with lightweight cardboard for individual soap slices.

Waves

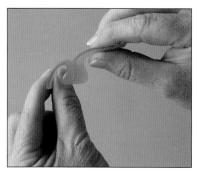

1. Repeat steps 1 and 2 of curls. Make a zig zag with fingers.

Tips

- Curls and Waves only work with transparent soap. Color soap White with powdered milk. (Do not use an opaque soap base.)
- Always place curls and waves in freezer or the shape may melt away in the hot base soap.

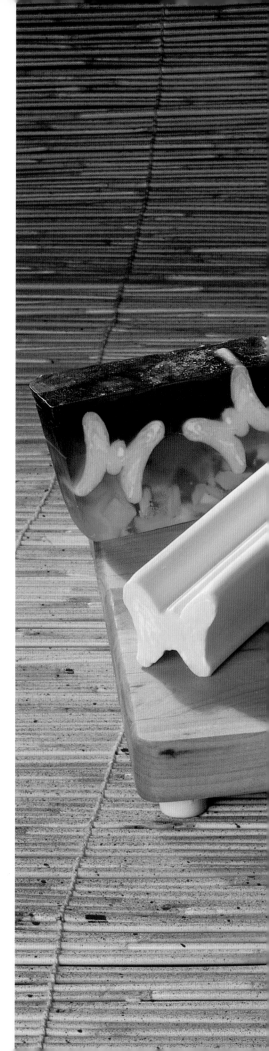

Surprise Loaf Soaps

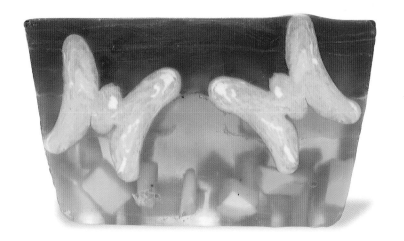

Butterfly Dance

Opaque Green and Light Yellow cubes, Soap Loft #06 butterfly. Float butterflies at different heights by layering background, gradating from Clear to Dark Blue.

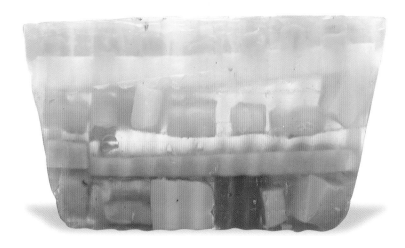

Stripes & Dots

$1/2$" Lime Green cubes, Pink sheet, White cubes, White sheet, small Lime Green cubes, Pale Yellow background.

Swirls

Red, Blue and Pale Yellow curls, Clear background.

Tips for Layered Soaps

• Create layered soaps by melting (include fragrance and color) some soap, and pour one layer of it into your mold. Let that start to set - in the mean time, melt (include fragrance and color) the next layer. When the first layer has a thick skin, and when the next layer is cooled a bit, spray the first layer with rubbing alcohol, and pour the second layer. You can repeat this with as many layers as you like!

• To embed soap chunks or soap shapes into a loaf of soap, melt the base soap and let it cool a bit. Spray or dip the soap chunks or soap shapes with rubbing alcohol and place chunk or shape in the mold. Then, when the base soap is starting to get thicker/cooler, pour this over the shape/chunks in the mold. Make sure to lift up the chunks/shapes once you pour the over-pour so that they are surrounded by soap.

• To prevent air bubbles between layers of soap, spray a light mist of rubbing alcohol on first layer after it has formed a skin, then pour next layer. For embedded items, immerse in alcohol before embedding in soap.

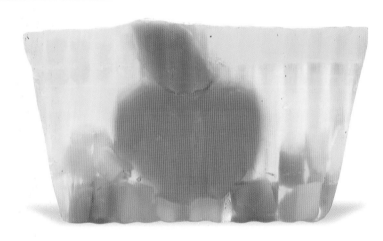

Apple

Transparent Red apple, Opaque Green, Yellow and White cubes, Clear background.

Sun & Sea

Opaque Yellow sun, Opaque White curl, Opaque Yellow cubes. Use Dark Blue background at bottom, allow to skin and add curl and sun. Pour Clear background to two-thirds full. Add cubes and fill to top.

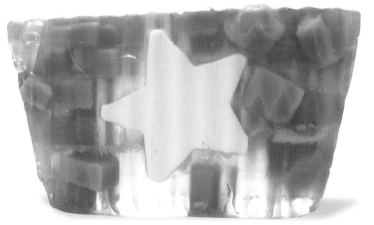

Star

Opaque White star, Opaque Blue cubes, Transparent Light Blue background.

Surprise Loaf Soaps

Smiley Face

Use ½" PVC pipe or small bottle to make Coffee soap slices for eyes. Shape Coffee soap wave for mouth. Freeze eyes and mouth. Layer with Opaque Yellow once before placing eyes and mouth.

Man in the Moon

White molded moon, 3 Yellow triangles. Place moon and triangles in circular mold and carefully pour Dark Blue background.

Palm Tree

Yellow cookie cutter animal, Green curls, Brown rectangle. Place in rectangular mold and pour Clear background.

Heart

Pink heart, Opaque Light Pink and Opaque White cubes. Pour Transparent Blue to Clear gradated background.

Noah's Ark

Opaque Peach molded boat. Pour Clear and Transparent Dark Blue simultaneously for sea and sky.

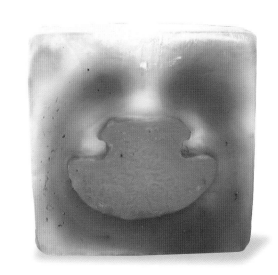

Leaf

Molded Opaque Green leaf, Transparent Red cubes. Pour Clear background with Yellow shavings. Sprinkle with oregano.

Surprise Loaf Soaps

Stained Glass

Cut Transparent Red, Green and Purple shapes, Opaque White background. Make several layers for placing shapes.

Cool Green Float

Opaque Light Yellow and Transparent Green cubes, Pale Yellow background.

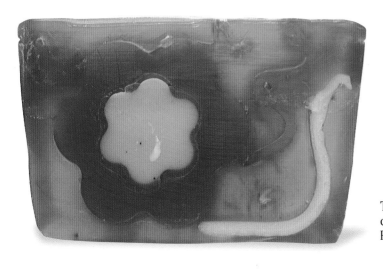

Red Flower

Transparent Red cookie cutter flower, Opaque Yellow cookie cutter center, Dark Green and White curls and waves, Pale Pink background.

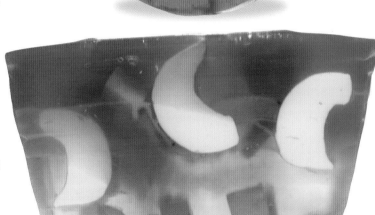

Gingerbread Boy

Dark Brown cookie cutter boy, Red cubes, Transparent Brown background.

Moon River

Opaque White moons, Opaque Yellow cubes. Pour Clear to Dark Blue gradated background.

Lips

Transparent Dark Red lips, Opaque White background.

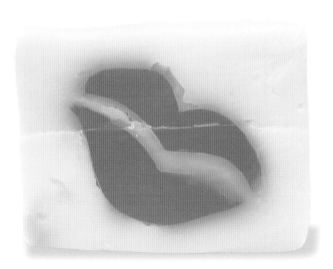

Holiday Loaves

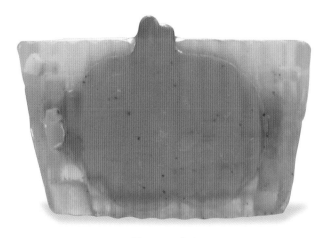

Pumpkin

Orange cookie cutter pumpkin, Opaque Lime Green and White cubes, Clear background with Yellow shavings and nutmeg sprinkles.

Holiday Red

1" Clear cubes stacked randomly, Transparent Red background.

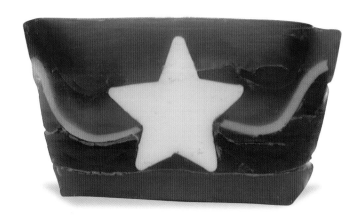

4th of July Star

White star, White wavy sheet, Transparent Dark Blue background.

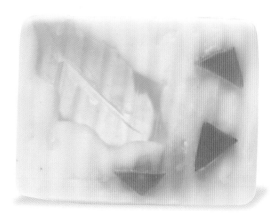

Holly Leaf

Transparent Green holly leaf, Transparent Red triangles, Opaque White background.

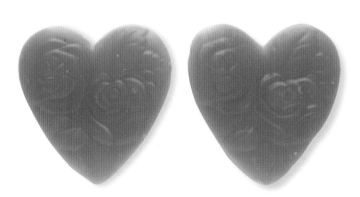

Valentine Hearts

Hearts molded from hand milled soap mixed with one tablespoon of strawberry purée.

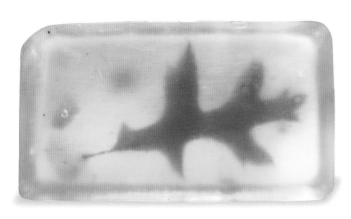

Natural Fall Leaf

Oak leaf, Transparent Red chunks, Opaque Light Green chunk, Transparent Green background with a dash of nutmeg.

Christmas Tree Loaf

Opaque Light Green cookie cutter tree, White wavy line. Pour background using Clear with glitter.

Easter Egg

Blow egg out of shell using a ¼" hole. Fill shell using paper funnel, allow to harden. Place in freezer to chill. Peel egg.

Christmas Tree

Transparent Green with glitter cookie cutter tree.

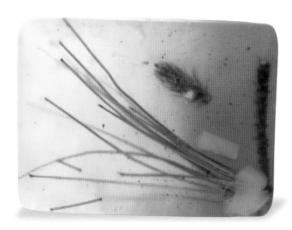

Pine Bar

Pine needles, Cone bud, Stem, Opaque Light Green chunks. Pour Clear and Clear with Brown and Green shavings simultaneously for background.

Historical Fun Fact

The power of scents was so exaggerated in eighteenth century England, that a law was passed during the reign of King George III in 1774 that stated, "All women, of whatever age, rank, profession, or degree whatever, virgins, maids, or widows, that shall from and after this act empower upon, seduce and betray into matrimony any of His Majesty's subjects by the use of scents, paints, cosmetics, washes, artificial teeth, false hair, Spanish wool [a kind of rouge], iron stays, hoops, high-heeled shoes, or bolstered hips, shall incur the penalty of the law now in force against witchcraft and like misdemeanors, and that the marriage, upon conviction, shall stand null and void."

Soap Shapes

Basic Hand Milled Soap Recipe

MATERIALS: ½ cup soap, 2 tablespoons water,
2 tablespoons olive oil, Color, Fragrance

Soap Snowman

1. Assemble ingredients: toothpick, oil, water and soap cubes. Premeasure oil, water and fragrances in bowls. Melt soap cubes. See page 10, steps 1 through 4 for details.

2. Roll three balls. Make one ball smaller for the head. Work as fast as possible while the soap is still pliable.

3. Use a toothpick to assemble the two larger balls first. Allow one end of the pick to stick out of the top to attach the head (about half way through the head).

4. Place eyes, nose and button in position using small colored strips of soap or hard candy and small buttons. Attach two small cinnamon sticks in the middle ball for arms.

Floating Soap

1. Use the Hand Milled Soap Recipe and place the melted soap in an electric mixer to fluff with air.
2. Just before hardening, form into molds or balls. The extra air causes the soap to float.

Soap on a Rope

MATERIALS: Basic Hand Milled Soap Recipe, 2 feet of braided cord
1. Tie knots in each end of the cord.
2. Fold cord in half and tie the 2 ends together.
3. Make the Soap Recipe and form ball around the rope. Make sure the rope ends are about three-quarters of the way into the ball.

Tip for Soap on a Rope

• Using a ball mold, make 2 halves around the rope to form a ball. If making large batches, beat the soap with an electric mixer.

Soap Dough

Fun for animal shapes! Kids love this one and maybe they'll get clean as they play.
Mix Floating Soap, adding ¼ cup of extra oil while stirring vigorously. This will make the soap more pliable. Use toothpicks to attach arms and legs. Color with food coloring, cinnamon, coffee and chocolate. Make sure children do not try to taste. You can wet the dough if it dries out or remelt and start over.

Soap Jewels

Using Method 1 in Soap Balls, form small balls and roll in shavings of colored soap. Place the soaps in Jewel bags for kids' gifts.

Soap Balls

Method 1 - Use the Hand Milled Soap Recipe. As it thickens while stirring, wet hands and form into a ball. Place on a rack to dry. This is a good way to use left over soap.
Method 2
1. Shave scraps in a bowl or use grated fresh soap.
2. Sprinkle water over the scraps, stir until soap softens.
3. Form into a ball. Squeeze all the air and water out.
4. Place soap on a rack to dry. Squeeze every day to tighten ball until it is completely dry. This may take a few days.

Baths
Fabulous and soothing, salts and oils add enjoyment and aid relaxation as you bathe.

Bath Oil Recipe

Combine all ingredients.
Wait at least a week before enjoying.
½ cup of almond oil
½ cup of castor oil or aloe vera
Oil from 6 to 8 Vitamin E capsules
Dried flowers
25 to 30 drops of fragrance

Bath Salts Recipe

Combine all ingredients in an airtight jar and shake every day for one week.
1 cup of Epsom salt
1 cup of sea or rock salt
Food coloring
20 drops of fragrance
Use ¼ cup per bath for a relaxing aromatic experience.

Milk Bath Recipe

1 cup of powdered milk
1 tablespoon of powdered
  Orris root or benzoin
½ cup of Epsom salt
½ cup of sea or rock salt
20 to 25 drops of fragrance

Bubble Bath Recipe

Combine all in airtight bottle.
3 cups of clear mild dishwashing detergent
6 to 8 vitamin E capsules
¼ cup of glycerin
25 to 30 drops of fragrance
Food coloring
Dried orange slices and orange peel

1. Measure Epsom and rock salt and pour into a bowl.

2. Add fragrance and stir.

3. Add color and mix until all salt is colored.

4. Add additional salt if mixture is too damp.

Soothing oils and salts make bath time truly a sensual experience. And these oils and salts have healing properties. Add scents and your bath time will become an aromatheraphy session.

BATH SALT

BATH OIL

MILKBATH

MILK BATH

BUBBLE BATH

SALT BATH

MILKY BATH

AloeVera Soap

Rose Milk

Wrapping for Gifts

*For unique and treasured gifts,
wrap your handmade soaps with imagination
or add them to gift baskets.*

Tips for Gift Wrapping

• Let your imagination be your guide!
• Use raffia, twine and shells to add a natural touch to your gifts.
• For a bit of glamour, tie mesh ribbon around a golden soap.
• Use a button to accent yarn tied around a stack of wrapped soap.